THE ROAD AHEAD

*Based on World Prophecies
of the Famed Indian Mystic
Paramhansa Yogananda*

Swami Kriyananda

D1603096

CRYSTAL CLARITY PUBLISHERS Commerce, California

© 2023, 1973 by Hansa Trust
All rights reserved. Published 2023
First Edition, 1973. Second Edition, 1974. Third Edition, 2023.
Printed in United States of America
  2 4 6 8 10 9 7 5 3 1

CRYSTAL CLARITY PUBLISHERS
1123 Goodrich Blvd. | Commerce, California
crystalclarity.com | 800.424.1055
clarity@crystalclarity.com

ISBN 978-1-56589-065-7 (print)
ISBN 978-1-56589-592-8 (e-book)

Cover artwork by Nayaswami Jyotish
Cover and interior layout and design by Crystal Clarity Publishers

The *Joy Is Within You* symbol is registered by Ananda Church
of Self-Realization in Nevada County, California.

CONTENTS

FOREWORD

Nearly fifty years have passed since this book was first published in 1973, but it might well have been written today. Swami Kriyananda writes here about a number of trends that are destined to bring about hard times socially and economically. More importantly, he shares predictions and prophecies that Paramhansa Yogananda made about challenges that lie before us now, and how best to weather the storm that is brewing on the horizon.

In a section called "Forewarned is Forearmed," Kriyananda writes:

> To try to pierce the veil and peer ahead in time is not always, as people often claim, utterly futile. Present signs often point at least to probable future developments. And especially in critical and insecure times such as these, it behooves us to do what we can to plan ahead intelligently. During other periods of great change in history there have always been men and women of foresight who managed to ride the storms to new heights of success, while others were crushed and broken by calamities for which they were totally unprepared.

We are now in the midst of the largest pandemic of our lives due to the coronavirus. While hundreds of thousands of lives will be lost, the virus itself will be tamed relatively soon. But the financial effects will last for years—perhaps for decades.

The same destructive economic forces that Paramhansa Yogananda and Swami Kriyananda warned about all those years ago are still present today. And they have grown increasingly powerful and dangerous in the intervening years.

What forces are we talking about? The most dangerous is greed, which Yogananda explained was "the root cause of financial depressions." A second is the tendency to spend beyond one's means. This exists in nations no less than individuals, and on a worldwide scale. People, nations, and an increasingly interconnected world are all spending more than they are earning.

This house of cards is built on an unstable foundation and will have to collapse at some point. The collapse will not be pleasant, especially for those who have not steeled their hearts, minds, and souls by the practice of right attitude and meditation.

Is this fate preordained and unavoidable? No, because everything that happens is caused by karma, in this case the karmic effects of current mass consciousness. If there were a change of consciousness (perhaps the virus will play a part in bringing about a positive change), this fate could be avoided. But the trends that Swami Kriyananda addresses have increased, not diminished, since this book was first published. Avoiding the results does not look promising.

A word on timing. Some readers may say, "The dire predictions given in this book have not yet come to pass. So why should we believe that they are still coming?' People of divine vision can clearly see the underlying, often hidden, forces in human nature. These forces are destined to produce certain results, but the timing is difficult to predict.

Think of it this way: Geologists study the increasing pressures of tectonic plates far beneath the surface of the earth. They can reliably predict that there will be an earthquake, but it's more difficult to say exactly when it will happen. We are most certainly headed toward such an economic and social earthquake. The "why" is evident, the "what" is looming, but the "when" is not as clear.

During the many years that we were with Swami Kriyananda there were several possible trigger points that seemed like the beginning of the social upheavals discussed in this book. Each time such points occurred, he would warn us to prepare for hard times, and in large part the Ananda communities have done so—both on practical and, more importantly, spiritual levels. We are in a strong position to reach out a helping hand to those who will need it.

That helping hand starts now—by sharing this book with you, and by warning you to prepare for social and economic upheaval while there is still some time remaining. The advice in *The Road Ahead* is like a spiritual vaccination: a little shot now can help you avoid much greater suffering in the future.

Ultimately, everything is in the hands of a loving God. The predictions that Paramhansa Yogananda made were not to frighten us, but to strengthen us to deal with what lies ahead. Even suffering has its divine purpose: to change those harmful habits that keep us imprisoned in lower consciousness. The best preparation of all is to deepen our inner life and attune our individual will with the will of God. Those who do so will come out of this period stronger and freer.

The Road Ahead can be our road map. It shows us how to move forward through the challenges and obstacles in our path toward new horizons of greater spiritual awareness and unity for humanity as a whole.

Nayaswami Jyotish and Nayaswami Devi
Spiritual Directors
Ananda Sangha Worldwide

THE ROAD AHEAD

*Based on World Prophecies
of the Famed Indian Mystic
Paramhansa Yogananda*

Chapter 1

THE NEED TO PREPARE

How will you and your family and friends fare in the years to come? Will you continue to eat well? to drive your own cars? to own your own homes? Will you still be able to vote in free elections? to choose your own line of work? to live and travel where you please? Are world wars now a thing of the past? Is mankind moving toward greater plenty, security, and social justice?

Or are we in a tailspin toward hunger, poverty, political slavery, global destruction and chaos?

Sweeping Changes

If ever there was a time when the future of the human race was in doubt, it is now. Man's sophistication in the techniques of destruction seems hardly to be outdistancing his willingness to destroy himself. Numerous scientists have stated that we are fast approaching a time of such over-population that our planet simply won't be able to produce enough food to feed everyone;

that within a very few years—quite possibly in the present decade—millions will starve to death, or be killed in global wars as nations strive to exploit the available food supplies. More and more reputable economists are predicting world-wide depression. Dwindling sources of energy threaten dire shortages of many of the prime necessities of modern life.

Whatever the future holds in store for us, one thing is certain: We may look forward to sweeping changes in our lives in the years to come.

Forewarned Is Forearmed

To try to pierce the veil and peer ahead in time is not always, as people often claim, utterly futile. Present signs often point at least to *probable* future developments. And especially in critical and insecure times such as these, it behooves us to do what we can to plan ahead intelligently. During other periods of great change in history there have always been men and women of foresight who managed to ride the storms to new heights of success, while others were crushed and broken by calamities for which they were totally unprepared.

Yet common sense was seldom the only guideline of those fortunate few. Many of them were led by a sort of sixth sense, an inner certainty of impending developments. It is as though, in times of widespread need, inspirations were sent to man from higher, spiritual realms: silent suggestions which a few sensitive people have been inwardly attuned to receive.

And not people only. Consider how often animals seem to know in advance when an exceptionally cold winter is due, or famine, or a record flood. Animals generally have been known to prepare for disasters of which human beings had no premonition. The squirrels have laid in larger stores of acorns; the beavers have built dams to higher levels.

When the time comes for new strides in civilization, too, more than one person often "chances" on the same discovery at the same time. It is as though the idea had been put into the atmosphere for all men to receive it who were prepared to do so. Paramhansa Yogananda, the great master of yoga and spiritual teacher from India, wrote that scientists are inspired by God to discover, at the right time and place, the secrets of His creation

Warnings and Promises

In every age, there have been a few saintly persons who were especially attuned to the subtle messages of inner, divine guidance. Especially in times of great danger to humanity, these persons have often raised their voices publicly in prophetic warning. Whoever heeded them was spared many of the affliction suffered by other men.

Our present age would seem to be such a time. Great seers have raised their voices to speak of coming calamities. At the same time, however, they have claimed to be able to see through the tunnel of approaching darkness to a landscape brighter and more beautiful than any in mankind's present memory. The trials they predict are, they say, a preparation for a better world, a necessary purification, and not merely a punishment for past sins.

At the same time, they have also offered us a present light to guide us through the tunnel, that the coming darkness may be lessened, even dispersed—if not by mankind generally, then at least by sensible individuals. If anyone cares to prepare wisely for the road ahead, he would do well to heed the words of warning, as well as of promise, of those great souls.

Chapter 2

PARAMHANSA YOGANANDA

(1893-1952 A.D.)

Of the great sages of our time whose concern for mankind has led them to make important world prophecies, one was Paramhansa Yogananda, author of the famous spiritual classic, *Autobiography of a Yogi*. Yogananda lived for over thirty years in the West, teaching and inspiring countless thousands of people. In 1925, in Los Angeles, he founded the headquarters of the still-flourishing organization, Self-Realization Fellowship, which now has numerous branch centers in many parts of the world.

Yogananda was chiefly concerned with the spiritual guidance of his students and disciples. Like many great teachers, however, he was also deeply concerned for the overall welfare of mankind. Indeed, he claimed that true spiritual teachings benefit man on every level of life, and not only the spiritual. Thus he sometimes spoke out firmly on matters of general, worldly import, though always with the deeper purpose of inspiring people to embrace spiritual values.

Like most great masters, Paramhansa Yogananda
never talked systematically or at length about the
future. Even to his disciples, when telling them
what to expect in their own lives, he rarely went
further than a brief sentence here, a hint there,
always unexpectedly offered. He wanted us to develop our own understanding, and not to depend
on him to do our thinking for us.

Nevertheless, he was a seer of such high spiritual
attainments that even his briefest comments were
worth more than long statistical analyses by so-
called experts. Past and future were as clear to him
as the present is to us. Two examples of his clair-
voyance might be interesting as an introduction to
those of his world prophecies which I, as his direct
disciple, managed to assemble over the three and a
half years that I spent with him.

India's Independence

When he was a young man, Yogananda, always remarkable for his dynamic energy, was approached
by a group of friends and urged to lead a revolu-
tionary movement for the liberation of India. He

declined, saying, "India will be freed during my lifetime by spiritual means." He then warned his friends that the weapons they were expecting to arrive by ship from Germany would be discovered by the British and confiscated. He urged the would-be revolutionaries to withdraw from active involvement before it was too late. But they ignored his advice, were caught after the weapons had been found and confiscated as predicted, and spent the next few years in prison. (Afterwards, several of them joined Mahatma Gandhi's non-violent "revolution" to free India.

The Reality of Christ

Some years later, in Boston, Massachusetts, the Master received a letter criticizing him for "sponsoring" Jesus Christ in the West. "Don't you know," the writer demanded, "that Jesus never lived? He was a myth invented only to deceive people." The writer had omitted to sign his name.

About a week later, Yogananda entered the Boston public library. Seeing a man seated on the bench under a window, he went over and joined him. Gently he inquired:

"Why did you write me that letter?"

The stranger almost jumped from his seat. "What do you mean?" He cried. "What letter?"

"The one in which you claimed that Jesus Christ was a myth."

"But—how did you know I wrote you that?"

"I have my ways," answered the Master, quietly. "But I wanted you to know that the same power which enabled me to find you enables me also to know that Jesus did live, and that he was indeed what the Bible says he was: a great Master, a true Christ."

Many statements in the following chapters were recorded by me personally from discussions with the Master. Others were taken from his lectures. A minority of them are secondhand, having been reported to me by some of my fellow disciples.

Chapter 3

DEPRESSION

To a large number of young Americans, depression is only a word. Older people in this country, however, who lived through the depression of the 1930s, still carry psychic scars: memories of unemployment, bread lines, loss of self-respect. Everyone would rather believe that such a disaster could never happen again.

The True Cause: Greed

Yet the seeds of depression are still here. The so-called "safeguards" with which our political leaders claim to have surrounded us are largely paper fortresses. There is no safeguard against human ignorance. There is no safeguard against greed. And the greed, born of human ignorance, is the true cause of every financial depression.

Paramhansa Yogananda saw another, even greater depression in store for us in our times. He was particularly concerned over the present-day economic philosophy of perpetual indebtedness. However much one tries to dignify excess spending in the name of "boosting the economy," the fact is no one can exist indefinitely in a state of financial over-extension without offending against certain basic realities. Living continually on money that one hopes to get "someday" has always in the end proved disastrous—as much so for nations as for individuals. In America today we are encouraged practically to *live* on the installment plan. And our government itself sets us the worst example: Presently it is in debt in the amount of nearly 500 billion dollars.

The Road to Inflation

When individuals over-extend themselves financially, their creditors end up seizing their possessions. When governments over-extend themselves, what do they do? They can usually defend themselves, at least against domestic creditors. But they can't afford to bite the hand that feeds them. Therefore they must take the alternate course of printing money with which to pay off their debts. This is paper money, with nothing to back it but more promises. The government's creditors, however, rarely object, for the pernicious effect of the inflation is not felt to begin with. They themselves get full value for their money when they spend it. It is only months later, as the new currency makes its way down to large masses of low-income people, that the full impact of the inflation becomes felt.

Paper Money Is Unstable

There was a man in Los Angeles a few years ago who used to pass out leaflets in the streets promoting what he called the sure cure for poverty. His solution? To get the government to print enough money to make everyone rich! Why, with enough paper dollars in circulation we'd all be millionaires.

The fallacy in his proposal was that paper money *in itself* is quite valueless. All it amounts to is an IOU from the government saying, in effect, "We have such-and-such a quantity of real treasure (usually gold or silver) to which this bill gives you a claim, should you wish to redeem it." A government can safely print up more such IOUs than the actual amount of solid wealth in its treasury, simply because it knows that people are very unlikely to want to reclaim all their money at once. *But it cannot afford to print up too many bills in ratio to its actual wealth.* When it does so, it merely inflates the currency.

For example, supposing our government were to act on that man's suggestion in Los Angeles and decide to erase poverty by making everyone in this country a paper-millionaire. Americans would respond by reasoning, "Well, if money's all that easily come by, then my strenuous labor and services are worth a great deal more of that kind of money." For a week's work people might end up demanding, and getting, billions of dollars—as in fact they did in Germany after World War I. There, a week's wages finally soared into the trillions of marks. Unfortunately, it also cost several million merely to ride the streetcar.

Energy: The True Wealth

The fact is that what paper money really represents is not even silver or gold, but energy. Gold is rare. It takes great effort to find and amass it. It is also, for a variety of reasons (beauty, easy workability, etc.), desirable enough to be universally acceptable as a medium of exchange.* But if gold were suddenly

---

* The barter system, frequently encountered in small, simply

discovered everywhere in vast and easily obtainable amounts, it would lose most of its value for us. *Energy* is humanity's real wealth. Perhaps the banks of the future will be backed directly by supplies of energy, convertible for use on farms, and in homes and factories. But for now, anyway, solid value for us human beings means something desirable which can be had only at the cost of exceptional effort. It cannot be something desirable but common, like air. Assuming a desirability that doesn't lose its glamor with the difficulty of attainment, we may state it as a definite principle:

The greater the expenditure of energy required to obtain a desired object, the greater its value for us.

And of course, conversely, the smaller the expenditure of energy required, the smaller the value for us.

---

structured societies, becomes impossibly cumbersome as a society grows larger and more complex. What could I offer you in exchange for an ear of corn, if all I possessed was a cow? Should I give you an ear of the cow? Or should I give you an IOU on that ear, against the time of the cow's eventual slaughter or death? And what could you do with such an IOU when dealing with someone who has never heard of me and my cow, and so could never actually claim the cow's ear?

Gold vs. National Productivity as Wealth

Our monetary system is based on gold. Economists have tried to free it from this basis by claiming that the nation's true wealth is its enormous productivity—in a sense, its output of human energy. This is of course true. Yet it is not true to practical purposes for the simple reason that the government does not (yet, at least) *own* that human energy. Nor (yet) does it own the factories, farms, and other channels for that energy. It has no right to use them for bargaining power. The government threatens our most basic political freedoms when it speaks of using the nation's productivity to support its solvency.

But so far, at least, the real basis of our monetary system is still gold, as our recent dollar devaluations amply demonstrate. And we are presently living far beyond our monetary means.

What Is Devaluation?

What about devaluation? How does it work? To reduce this question to the simplest possible terms, let us suppose I buy fifty cases of chocolate from you in Switzerland, paying you in American dollars. You then buy a comparable value in Coca-Cola from me in America, paying me in Swiss francs. Dollars are more useful to me in America than Swiss francs; francs are more useful to you in Switzerland than dollars. After our transaction, therefore, we can simply exchange currencies; neither of us will be the loser.

But suppose I buy fifty cases of chocolate from you and you buy a comparatively small amount of Coca-Cola. In this case, you'll have more dollars than I'll have of Swiss francs. For a time you may think, "Well, things will balance themselves out in time." But if this balance of trade continues to be lopsided, there may come a time when you say, "Look here, your dollars are only paper IOUs, anyway, for the real wealth you've been holding for me. I can't go on indefinitely paying my chocolate suppliers with promises. Therefore I'm going to have to ask you to send me some real wealth in exchange for these dollar IOUs."

Supposing at that point I reply, "I'm sorry, but I've written you IOUs on more wealth than I actually have." In this case, you might fight me and take from me by force the equivalent of my debt. Or you might refuse to do business with me again. Or, if it means enough to you to keep those supplies of Coca-Cola flowing (let's assume your chocolate workers need Coca-Cola to keep them awake while they're making chocolates), you may say, "Very well, but from now on, to equalize our trade imbalance, I'll require more dollars from you when you buy my chocolate, and I'll pay you fewer Swiss francs for your Coca-Cola." In effect, you'll be telling me that my currency is so inflated that you'll consider each paper dollar to be worth less of my gold; otherwise, it's no business between us in future. If I accept, then my dollars will have been devalued in relation to your francs.

This is in fact what has already happened to the U.S. dollar abroad. Presently there are some 45 billion paper dollars in central banks around the world. Another 30 billion paper dollars are held in different countries by private corporations. Add this total of $75 billion to our present national debt of $462 billion, and you get a staggering *total* indebtedness of 537 billion dollars! But we have only about $10 billion in gold in our treasury, and virtually no silver left at all as an alternate source of wealth. In the sixties, other countries began requesting so much of our gold in exchange for their paper dollars that at last we decided to stop the outflow of our rapidly dwindling reserves. President Nixon took the dollar off the gold standard. Now the dollar is officially backed by nothing but promises. Considering that we didn't keep our old promises, other nations have every reason to worry about how well we'll keep our new ones.

Actually, however, we tacitly admitted the dollar's real basis was gold when we devalued it in relation to other currencies. For we submitted to their evaluation of the problem, which was in effect to say, "If our $75 billion are backed by only $10 billion in gold, then the paper dollar is worth a great deal less to us than it has been in the past."

The Effects of Devaluation

Dollar devaluation abroad affects us in much the same way as inflation affects us at home. For we rely on foreign imports to keep our own business flowing. When we must pay more for those imports, we must charge more also for the goods we sell domestically.

Of course, we may turn to cheaper (and in many cases, less desirable) second choices at home, but it will be difficult to do so in the matter of basic raw materials for which we depend on overseas suppliers.

Of course also, exports will bring us correspondingly greater profits, since the foreign money we bring in will now be worth more.

But the net effect, after an initial stimulus to the economy, is on the one hand a surge of shortages at home as much-needed domestic supplies are sent abroad in search of greater profits; and on the other, a shortage, or a rise in the cost, of foreign goods and raw materials on which our economy has come to depend. True, the balance of payments may be improved, but only temporarily. In the long run devaluation is self-defeating.

Put in the simplest possible terms, how can one best improve his bargaining position? Either by having more wealth at his disposal, or, lacking that, by making his own products more desirable. Of various ways to increase the desirability of these products, an offer to sell them to the reluctant buyer at a lower cost is probably the worst, for it tells him, "I need you more than you need me."

But to try to improve one's position by offering also—with no more actual wealth at one's disposal—to pay more for the other person's goods in return, or to be forced by him to pay more for them: well, what can he possibly conclude? Surely this: that he has you over a barrel. If he doesn't take full advantage of such a situation, it means he's either a fool or a saint. Americans have been on the strong side of this equation too long not to appreciate the disadvantages of being on the weaker side.

Further Devaluation and Inflation Inevitable

With an enormous, and ever-growing, national debt (at present its amount is higher than *the sum of* indebtedness of all other countries in the world); with vast amounts of paper dollars abroad, and a continuing imbalance of trade with other countries; with increasing loss of faith abroad in the real strength of the dollar; and with a pathetically small amount of gold in our treasury in ratio to the number of dollars in circulation at home and abroad, the squeeze on the dollar has become enormous. Further dollar devaluations are inevitable. Further inflation is inevitable. If within the next one to five years we get away with the dollar being worth one-fifth of its present value, we may consider ourselves fortunate.

How Will You Be Affected?

Imagine now what will happen to you if the stock market crashes again, as it did in 1929; or if inflation gets really out of hand. Most people, living as they do on the installment plan, are in debt several times the total amount of their savings. They could easily be made penniless overnight.

What of Insured Savings?

But what of people who have those much-touted "insured" savings accounts, which are supposed to keep them from going bankrupt even if the banks fail? Well, in fact those accounts could be a major factor in helping to precipitate a run-away inflation. People don't realize that although their savings are insured up to $20,000 by the Federal Deposit Insurance Corporation, the actual amount of money backing their savings is only 1¼% of the total amount of insured deposits in America: $4 billion, to cover a total of $313 billion in savings (according to the FDIC 1969 Annual Report). If a few banks fail, the government will be able to bail their depositors out. But if large masses of people decide they need their money to meet rising expenses, the Federal Reserve Bank will have little choice but to pay off those insured savings in the only way left to it: by simply printing the necessary paper money to meet the demand. The more money they print in this way, the less those precious savings will be worth.

Yogananda's Predictions

Paramhansa Yogananda foresaw depression of massive proportions—far worse, he said, than that of the thirties. Indeed, from his various statements my impression was that he considered the depression of the thirties only the first rumblings of greater troubles to come.

"Americans," he said in February, 1945, "were growing so rich they forgot God. But now God is performing an operation. They will have only half as much wealth.

"But," he added, "they will be more spiritual."

In the last few years of his life he repeatedly warned his audiences that a time of great financial tribulation was coming.

"There will be great upheavals and unemployment in America," he told them. And again:

"The time is growing short. You have no idea of the sufferings that await mankind!"

"A terrible depression is coming, *far worse than the last one!*"

He must have foreseen a complete breakdown of many aspects of governmental management and control, for he also said, "Millions will die." Yet he may have been referring to death by other causes than starvation.

A fellow disciple of mine quoted the Master as telling her, "Money won't be worth the paper it is printed on."

And while speaking on the subject one Sunday morning in church, he cried with deep feeling, "You don't know what a terrible cataclysm is coming!"

Chapter 4

NATURAL CATACLYSMS

From the Master's last-quoted statement, my inference is that he was referring to the coming depression. This, at any rate, was the main gist of his public warnings in those days. Yet I must admit that my impression for a long time was that he may have been referring to some kind of natural catastrophe, certainly widespread, possibly even global.

A number of modern seers, notably Edgar Cayce,[*] have foreseen global cataclysms in the decades to come: a shifting of the earth's axis, the sinking of large land masses, the rising of others. So far as I know, Yogananda's comments on such matters were more than usually veiled. Had I known of those other predictions during his lifetime, I would certainly have asked him his opinion of them. But even assuming that he foresaw the same dangers, it is not likely that he would have dwelt on them. His main concern was to warn people in matters where positive preventive action was possible.

[*] The famous "sleeping prophet" of Virginia Beach. Cayce's predictions have often proved amazingly accurate.

Nevertheless, his brief reference to a "terrible cataclysm" might well be taken as a corroboration of others' predictions of world-upheavals. That large land masses can disappear in an instant he as much as said, for he endorsed the ancient legend of Atlantis, and of its sudden disappearance. He often said also that natural catastrophes, such as floods, famines, and earthquakes, can be triggered by disturbances in the mass consciousness of mankind. And he remarked that many such catastrophes would certainly be part of the general sufferings of the human race in the decades to come.

Yogananda's Predictions

He did, however, say something which, to me, hints at the possibility of global cataclysm in the years ahead. It may have been in answer to someone's remark on the cold winters in Boston. At any rate, the Master's comment, as it has been reported to me, was, "In the next century Boston will have a tropical climate, and the people there will be brown skinned."

Chapter 5

COMMUNISM

In Fatima, Portugal, in 1917 three children were told by the Virgin Mary, in a now-famous vision, that communism was destined to spread in all lands. Paramhansa Yogananda made an identical prediction. He added, however, that communism ultimately will be defeated by America.

Communism—Pros and Cons

Certain aspects of communism, of course, appeal to genuine humanitarian feelings. To feel active concern for one's fellow man, and to discourage people from clambering to success over the broken backs of their competitors; to pay heed to the sufferings of the poor and the unfortunate: such attitudes are not only desirable, but *necessary* if humanity is to rise to new *heights* of civilizations. But modern communism labors under the delusion that compassion can be produced, like automobiles, by the right kind of system, instead of by the inner, creative awareness of individuals. Communism views men as machines, to be shoved and molded into whatever pattern is deemed best by the country's leaders for the efficient functioning of the State. Communism discourages personal initiative, idealism, and conscience: qualities, in short, without which no man can rise above the animal level. On the other hand, communism encourages inertia, herd-consciousness, and similar, spiritually soporific attitudes which can only contribute to man's degeneration. Unlike active, personal concern on a local level, massive, bureaucratic handling of even the most worthy programs breeds inefficiency, cynicism, and incredible waste.

Communism Breaks Its Promises

There may be some virtue in modern communism as a means of quickly coordinating societies that are helplessly mired in the past. In the long run, however, the pretensions of modern communists are fraudulent. They offer universal brotherhood, but bring men universal suspicion and fear. They talk of human dignity, but treat individuals with contempt. They promise everyone security, but give people, if anything, the security of cattle. They proclaim freedom from want, but ignore man's deeper, spiritual wants: his natural hunger for wisdom, for personal fulfillment, and for following his own inner lights in seeking that fulfillment. Even in achieving their materialist goals, their top-heavy system makes them inept and inefficient.

Communism Is Atheistic

But by far the worst aspect of modern communism is the overt stand it takes against God and against all spiritual values. If in nothing else, in this alone communism would stand opposed to everything in man that gives him hope of progress toward ultimate perfection.

Humanity's Supreme Threat

Yogananda saw atheistic communism as the supreme threat to humanity in this Twentieth Century. To him, the true struggle on earth has always been between cosmic forces of light and of darkness. In these present times it is especially so. Men and nations that serve high and noble ideals, or that actively spread ignoble materialism and irreligion, unconsciously act as instruments of these great forces. Communism, the Master said, far more so than most people realize, is an instrument of the satanic power.

After World War II the world was shocked to learn of the sufferings that had been endured by prisoners in the Nazi concentration camps. But the Master several times remarked:

"Hitler was a Boy Scout compared to Stalin!"

The Method: Attack by Subversion

"When," I once asked him, "will Russia attack us?"

"First," he replied, "they will try from within."

How did he foresee that they would go about their endeavor? by propaganda? by political or economic sabotage? by open revolution? So far as I know, he never said. But in a modern climate of tolerance for others' political beliefs—and no one I ever met was more open and loving towards all men than he was—I remember how sternly and forcefully he spoke against communist treachery from within our own ranks. His concern was the more striking because his mission was devoted to bringing people to God, and not to leading them toward a better worldly life. Yet he felt the danger to *dharma* (righteousness) to be so great as to merit a warning in the strongest possible terms.

"You must report people," he cried, "if you know them to be communists. Do not allow them to betray this great country."

I am sure he would have deplored the indiscriminate "witch hunts" of the fifties, had he lived through that era. Yet he would have deplored just as much the fact that the irresponsible accusations of Senator McCarthy and others inevitably caused a public reaction to the point where communists nowadays are allowed to work more or less openly. Time and again, any effort to oppose them has been widely decried in the name of tolerance and fair play. Communists themselves, as the Master pointed out, don't believe in fair play; it is part of their actual creed to reject it. (Witness Russia's ruthless suppression of rebels in Hungary and Czechoslovakia. Witness also the fact that, once communists gain control of a country, the first thing they do is kill off the intellectuals who paved the road for their victory by defending their right to fair play.) We are either weak or foolish, but certainly not spiritual when we pretend that communists will surely play fair if we do, just because it's nice.

Lesser Tactics of Subversion

How *would* the communists go about undermining us from within?

By revolution? That hasn't been their usual tactic so far, in countries much smaller and less powerful than ours. It is most improbable that they will try it here, unless it be only as a diversionary tactic. In fact, they have already stated that America would not need to be conquered by force.

By propaganda? Well, surely at least that. It isn't difficult these days to interest people in systems as a solution to human problems, and communism represents the very apotheosis of The System. Intellectuals especially pride themselves on being above petty, human prejudices, and therefore are an easy prey to concepts that treat people as mere statistics. But can anyone seriously believe that dedicated communist would give such a low priority to America's conversion that they'd be content with taking mere verbal pot shots at us?

Consider the oft-reiterated intention of communist leaders to bring all nations under their political sway. They've never made any secret of this intention. Moreover, they've acted on it consistently. It would be naive to dismiss their words as mere rhetoric.

Consider then the fact that only one country on earth stands as any real obstacle to the fulfillment of their ambitions: America. No strategic genius is needed to guess they will do their level best to remove this obstacle. People who have not stopped at subversion elsewhere will most certainly consider mere propaganda a weapon of secondary importance in America.

The Subversion of Power

What methods, then, are they most likely to favor? Candle-lit basements, bewhiskered men with foreign accents, gnashing teeth, and fanatical stares dimly visible through dark glasses? Not if they have any brains at all.

But the question requires no argument. One need only study communist methods elsewhere in the world, where success has finally brought them out into the open. Or simply put yourself in their shoes. Obviously, a nation is run, not from wine cellars and dank basements, but from the top pinnacles of power. It is those places that communists must try, and in fact always *have* tried, to infiltrate.

The Likelihood of Success

The next, and more serious, question then is: What is to prevent them from succeeding? The high positions in this country are not filled by people whom, over their modest objections, Americans have drafted by popular acclaim. Our leaders rather, from a variety of motives, have always actively *sought* high positions for themselves. It *stands* to the simplest reason that, given a number of gifted, intelligent communists determined to secure high posts for themselves in a democracy, some of them, at least, will succeed.

As a matter of fact, an attitude of attack almost inevitably generates more energy than one of general complacency, prodded by a little personal ambition. Given the same degree of talent and intelligence as his opponent, the conspirator's chances of success in the political arena are likely to be greater. All he need do is pass himself off as a nice, dedicated, responsible citizen with nothing but the welfare of his country at heart. It needn't even be all that much of an act. We must credit some communists, at least, with the belief that they *are* working for the welfare of their fellow man, and even of this country.

The Threat to Our Currency

Now, where will they work the hardest to penetrate? Into government circles? Into the media, where they can subtly mold public opinion? They'd be foolish not to try both. But thoughtful people must be particularly concerned, in view of our suicidal fiscal policies in recent decades, that they may have focused some of their heaviest energies on the U.S. monetary structure.

Communists have never been shy about announcing their long-range intentions. And they have always shown a remarkable tenacity to their original plans. To debauch the currency of America seems to have been their intention from the start. At any rate, in addition to the high priority they have always given to America's "conversion," John Maynard Keynes, the famous economist, and a careful student of such matters, wrote:

Lenin is said to have declared that the best way to destroy the Capitalist System was to debauch the currency. By a continuing process of inflation, governments can confiscate, secretly and unobserved, an important part of the wealth of their citizens . . . Lenin was certainly right. There is no subtler, no surer means of overturning the existing basis of society than to debauch the currency. The process engages all the hidden forces of economic law on the side of destruction and does it in a manner which not one man in a million is able to diagnose.*

Will There be a Revolution?

One time Paramhansa Yogananda was told of some new building restrictions that had been imposed by city hall. Sighing, he remarked half jestingly, "There ought to be a revolution!"

After a pause, he added with sudden seriousness, "There *will* be one."

---

* John Maynard Keynes, *Economic Consequences of the Peace* (1919), pp. 235f. Quoted in Robert L. Preston, *How to Prepare for the Coming Crash* (Hawkes Publications, Salt Lake City, Utah, 1973, p. 114.

He was against governmental interference in people's lives in the name of concern for their physical needs. His opinion of many of the reforms of the thirties was, I must admit, not high. Did he consider this modern trend a sign of communist influence? Did he believe it would reach such proportions—perhaps as a result of severe depression—that only a revolution would save America from the fate of countries now under communist domination? He didn't say, but the implications in what he did say are worth thinking over.

Chapter 6

WORLD WARS AND THE FATE OF NATIONS

Is the world fated to be embroiled in another war? If a few prophets can see into the future, does this mean that nations are doomed to destruction, or destined for greatness, by some Will higher than their own?

According to some of mankind's most ancient teachings, there *is* a law governing the affairs of men. It is only that, however: a law, not some cosmic hand whimsically writing off fates for us over which we, poor pawns, have no say whatever. The name for this law is *Karma*. Karma is the root principle from which the Newtonian law of action and reaction derives. According to karmic law, every action, even on the subtlest levels of thought, sooner or later attracts to itself a relative reaction. Newton's Law of Motion states: "To every action there is always an equal and contrary reaction." This is merely a rediscovery on a physical level of a truth which ancient *rishis* (sages) long ago found applied to human affairs and to life in general.

The more conscious and deliberate an action, the greater its power to attract to itself a like result. Good deeds, for example, performed absent-mindedly bring almost off-handedly good results. But good deeds done out of deep love return great blessings to the doer. There is, in fact, no such thing as good or bad "luck." The good and bad that descend on us are purely the results of previous causes.

Yet not all of these causes were created by ourselves, even when it is we who enjoy or suffer their effects. There is mass karma as well as individual karma. One form of mass karma is that created by nations. As Americans, whatever karma our country has spun for itself as a whole, we who live here must bear the consequences of it.

There are of course ways of mitigating the results of bad karma, whether individually or as a nation. By setting up powerful enough good waves of thought or of action, one may lessen the effects of previous mistakes. But the law is a universal fact of nature; it is not the fancy of a few ingenious minds that were committed to rationalize a set of sectarian presuppositions. As St. Paul said: "Be not deceived; God is not mocked; for whatsoever a man soweth, that shall he also reap" (Galatians 6:7).

A prophet, when he sees what is in store for men or for nations, is seeing the fruits of their own individual or collective actions. These "destinies" are not absolutely foreordained. Selfless love, and strict adherence to the principles of *dharma* (the path of righteousness) can change these destinies if they are bad; can improve them, if they are only moderately good. No prophecy should be accepted in a spirit of helpless acquiescence.

In this spirit, then, let us consider Paramhansa Yogananda's predictions as they pertain to the international scene. As regards specific nations, I recorded the following predictions:

America

America, he said, has acquired far more good karma than bad. This country will, in the end, prove invincible. For, as the Indian Scriptures say, "*Yata dharma, tata jaya*—where there is righteousness, there is victory." But Americans as a whole must enter the struggle more consciously on the spiritual side, otherwise they will face purification through great suffering. The coming depression will serve the deeper purpose of freeing Americans from excessive dedication to materialism.

England

I once asked the Master about the future of England. "England," he replied, "is finished"—finished, I'm certain he meant, as a major world power. From his remarks I gather that selfishness was her undoing. But he often praised the character of the British. "The reason Mahatma Gandhi's methods worked," he told us, "is that the British are gentlemen. Don't imagine that you will be able to win Russia by the same means. Only by great spiritual power could you tame a hungry, man-eating tiger. Otherwise you'd be practicing your non-violence in the tiger's stomach! Darkness must always be combatted positively—with love if possible, but the Scriptures also enjoin active warfare in a righteous cause, and this is a righteous cause." The Master referred, of course, to defensive warfare only, and to warfare without hatred of the enemy.

France and Japan

Of France he said, "The French have been too pleasure-loving, and for that they will have to suffer. But they are a good people. In the end they will come out well."

Japan, he said, will have to pay the price for attacking China in the 1930's. Its retribution will be that China will end up absorbing Japan.

India and America

India and America, representing respectively the harmonious development of man's spiritual and material natures, will join hands to lead the world to a life of balance and progress the like of which has not been seen in recorded history.

But the path to that happy era will not be an easy one.

More World Wars

A third world war, probably in the 1970's, will bring much of the free world under the banner of modern-day communism. The Master mentioned Russia, China, India, and Germany as being involved, but didn't, so far as I know, include America. Was this omission accidental? Or would economic depression here remove us, so to speak, from the arena? In fact, would a depression in America embolden China and Russia to settle their differences without fear of interference from us?

Toward the last decade of this century, he said, there will be still another, a fourth world war. At that time America will stand almost alone against the rest of the world. During that war, the Master said, "No corner on earth will be safe." This will be truly a purging by fire. "Europe," he once remarked, "will be devastated. Russia will be annihilated."

Victory and Peace

From this fourth world war America will emerge victorious—if victory we can call the outcome of such havoc. The old world will have been virtually destroyed. A new world will emerge, phoenix-like, from the ashes.

Thereafter mankind, sick to the marrow of warfare, will know peace and prosperity for hundreds of years.

Chapter 7

PLANETARY EVOLUTION

The great events of our times form part of a much broader, divine drama.

Swami Sri Yukteswar, Yogananda's great guru, explained in his book, *The Holy Science*,* an ancient Indian tradition that our sun moves not only in an orbit around the galaxy, but also in a relatively small orbit of 24,000 years around its stellar dual. Powerful rays of spiritual energy pour from our galactic center. As, in our 24,000-year orbit, we approach this galactic center, its powerful rays vitalize men's nervous systems, making them more sensitive to subtle, spiritual realities. As we draw farther away, mankind as a whole grows increasingly dull, less spiritually perceptive, more identified with matter and with all that such a limited identity connotes.

Ascending and Descending Ages

Here is not the place to present the archaeological

---

* Self-Realization Fellowship (Los Angeles), pp. vii–xix.

and historic evidence (it is considerable) in support of this ancient belief. I intend doing so at length in my book, *India's Ancient Book of Prophecy*,[†] when I can find the time to complete it. For now, let it suffice to say that the ancients described eight ages: four ascending and four descending on the scale of spiritual awareness. For 12,000 years from the point farthest from our galactic center, man passes through a dark age of 1,200 years, known as *Kali Yuga*, when it is difficult for him to think beyond solid, material realities; then an age of 2,400 years, known as *Dwapara Yuga*, when he develops the sensitivity to perceive the subtle nature of matter as energy; then an age of 3,600 years, *Treta Yuga*, when he develops the awareness that all things are essentially composed of thought; and finally an age of 4,800 years, called *Satya* or *Krita Yuga*, when he lives more perfectly in the realization that all is Spirit.

The descending ages reverse this development, from 4,800 years of descending *Satya Yuga* to

[†] Kriyananda did publish a book by that title, but didn't address this subject there. Instead, years later, he encouraged two Ananda members to write such a book, and gave it high praise: Joseph Selbie and David Steinmetz, *The Yugas: Keys to Understanding Our Hidden Past, Emerging Present and Future Enlightenment* (Crystal Clarity Publishers, Nevada City, 2010). —Publishers' note

3,600 of *Treta*, to 2,400 of *Dwapara*, to 1,200 of *Kali*.

Ours an Ascending Age

The lowest point in this 24,000-year cycle, Sri Yukteswar said, was reached in the year 499 A.D. 1,200 years from that time placed the end of the ascending *Kali Yuga* in the year 1699 A.D. In that year, he said, the solar system entered the ascending age of *Dwapara Yuga*, a period when mankind generally would succeed in penetrating the mysteries of matter, and would become increasingly aware of deeper realities, developing a sense of the underlying oneness of all life.

Between each *Yuga* (age) and the next there is a bridge—one hundred years in the case of *Kali Yuga*, two hundred in that of *Dwapara*, three hundred for *Treta*, and four hundred for *Satya Yuga*. Thus, *Dwapara Yuga* began only partially in 1699 A.D., but *fully* in 1899, at the turn of the present century. It was only six years later that Einstein published the three papers that revolutionized man's concept of the physical universe and laid the foundation for the atomic age. In this Twentieth Century we have

already seen the fufillment of much that Sri Yukteswar, writing in 1894, predicted. Matter is now
known to be energy. There is a new and growing
consciousness of human brotherhood, of the dignity and rights of all classes and nations. So-called
"backward" areas of the world have achieved new
stature as nations. One hears a growing demand for
international unity and peace. Warfare for glory is a
thing of the past.

The ancient prophecies of India, as explained by
Sri Yukteswar, support the more hopeful view that
the present state of world unrest presages not doom
but eventual adjustment to more spiritual values.
At present, mankind is like a growing child whose
old clothes are bursting at the seams. Old attitudes
and institutions, legacies from the dark age of *Kali
Yuga*, are too narrow to accommodate the expansive
spirit of *Dwapara*. Once we have learned to cast off
our old mental "clothes," we shall know peace and
true prosperity on every level of life.

Chapter 8

CAN SUFFERINGS BE AVOIDED?

Is it still possible to avoid the sufferings that have been foreseen? Yes, of course, if man accepts willingly the vibrations of the new age and ceases from clinging to those of the old. Yes, if men will but learn to love their fellow human beings selflessly, and substitute an attitude of service and cooperation for selfish greed and egotistical competition.

Unfortunately, these are big "ifs." Mankind as a whole seldom listens to its great spiritual teachers until the time of trial has already passed.

Individual Protection Possible

Individually, however, we *can* embrace the new-age consciousness. Even if we do so on this personal basis, we, at least, shall be spared much of the suffering with which the rest of the world is threatened. This is what Yogananda meant when he told people, "Those who follow this teaching will be protected." He was referring less, I am sure, to the sectarian aspects of his mission than to the universal path of spiritual awareness which he and other masters in our time have pointed out.

Safety Through Spiritual Awakening

It follows, then, that the greatest thing we can do for our fellow man, as well as for ourselves, is to serve as instruments of the Divine, and to help each of us in this little way, to bring about a spiritual awakening on earth.

It follows also that those who believe in spiritual values should support one another in a spirit of divine brotherhood. Sectarian squabbles dilute the one, most basic purpose of religion, which is to turn people to God. The true enemy of every church, of every religion is not the way some other church or religion interprets divine love, eternal life, or the instruments of grace. The enemy, rather, is man's delusion that matter circumscribes his realities, and that the animal from which he has evolved is all he is or ever can be.

Many of the sufferings that threaten humanity will be lessened if religious people will learn to cooperate with one another instead of competing to get as many people into their particular camps as possible.

Chapter 9

THE RELIGION OF THE FUTURE

Paramhansa Yogananda once said, "You are on the eve of a great spiritual awakening, a great change in the churches, where true souls will be drawn to seek the actual experience of God's presence."

Religious institutionalism belongs to *Kali Yuga*. So long as matter was conceived as solid and immutable, thought too was encased in human institutions. Mankind generally could think only in concrete terms. But the religion of the new age will be Self-realization—the search for God within one's own self,* and no longer the old dependence on dogmas, institutional proclamations, and priestly intercession.

Techniques of God-Communion

The principle "ritual" of the future will be meditation and God-communion, through such advanced techniques of mental unfoldment as Kriya Yoga

* As Jesus Christ said, "The kingdom of God is *within*" (Luke 9:21).

(the great meditative science which Paramhansa Yogananda was commissioned by his guru to bring to the West). The religion of the future will be non-sectarian. Direct experience of spiritual truth will replace formal creeds as the true test of religious life.

Chapter 10

THE SOCIAL PATTERN OF THE FUTURE

"Spiritual Socialism"

Paramhansa Yogananda said that society in future will be based in what he called "spiritual socialism." From this remark I gather that some of the ideals, even if few of the practices, of modern communism *are* in harmony with the vibrations of the new age, and to some extent explain why communism has gained such a hold on the minds of men.

I can give only my own interpretation of what the Master meant by this term, "spiritual socialism," since he didn't explain it. It is an interpretation, however, based on several years of direct association with him, during which time, although not everything he said was remembered, the *sense* of what he said lingered on, and lives within me still to this day.

Not Government-Directed

That aspect of communism which seeks to enslave people while providing for their material needs was certainly contrary to the Master's vision of justice. In principle, he was opposed even to social charities, because, he said, they discourage people from developing their own initiative. He deplored the direction taken by America during the last depression, when people learned to depend on the government to feed and look after them. This trend, which has only been gathering momentum, weakens the individual, and encourages the government to assume more and more the role of dictating men's personal lives. Such a trend is contrary to the entire principle of Self-realization.

Voluntary Cooperation

Since Yogananda's vision of the future included the removal of such social injustices, spiritual socialism as he envisioned it cannot imply some far-reaching socio-economic system, with the rigid controls that total government ownership would entail. Rather, it can only describe a society in which people have learned at last to think *naturally* in terms of "the greatest good for the greatest number." It implies a social condition in which people understand that more can be accomplished by voluntary cooperation with one another than by ceaseless, cut-throat competition. Therefore it implies, I think, a state where decentralization is seen to be as necessary to the country as centralization—each serving as an important counterbalance to the other.

For centralization of course there must be, in an age of such rapid transportation and communication as we live in already. Without some central management there would be chaos. But lest too much power be concentrated in the hands of a few men, it is also desirable that man's deeper values rest on human and spiritual, not on political considerations. It is one thing to be expected to abide by the same traffic laws wherever one goes. It is quite another to be told where he may go.

World Brotherhood

Under spiritual socialism, then, there will be universal equality based on common acceptance rather than on government-enforced laws. At the same time, Yogananda foresaw a united states first of Europe and, separately, of the Americas, then eventually a united states of the world.

Chapter 11

COOPERATIVE COMMUNITIES

In conjunction with his warnings of a coming depression, Paramhansa Yogananda repeatedly urged his listeners to band together in cooperative spiritual communities, to buy land together out in the country and there to live simply, close to nature and to God, guided by the twofold principle of "plain living and high thinking." Such communities, he said, would serve as models for the new age, when countless similar, self-sustaining communities will popularize voluntary cooperation over competition as the true key to lasting prosperity and inner fulfillment.

So urgent was he in his efforts to get people to act on his advice that, during his lectures, he would cry, "In this way you will have the best kind of job. You will be working for yourselves!" Then, in reference to such jobs, he would have us affirm loudly after him: "Job means peace! happiness! freedom!"

Ananda Cooperative Village

I have described this community concept in detail in my book, *Cooperative Communities—How to Start Them, and Why*. Therein I have described also a community, Ananda Cooperative Village, which I myself founded several years ago in the foothills of the Sierra Nevada near Nevada City, California, where Paramhansa Yogananda's communitarian ideal is practiced by over one hundred full-time residents. If you are interested in this vitally important subject, I suggest you obtain this book and study it carefully.

A Counter-Balance to Federalism

Cooperative communities of the future, the Master said, will exist everywhere. They will be placed, as Ananda is now, where people will gather for commonly held, high-minded purposes, and not only for economic security. They will serve as an important balance to governmental centralization, and will to a great extent relieve the governments of the world of the burden of caring for the sick and the aged; for such communities would naturally look after their own.

Imagine, if you will, a nation bound together under a central government, yet having thousands of separate, self-sustaining, intentional villages (how different from the average, unplanned and omni-directional modern community!) where many of the practical functions of government would be handled by people known intimately by their constituents, and knowing their constituents in return. In such a system, bureaucracy would be held at a minimum.

A Doorway to the World

Such villages would not be isolated from the rest of the world, as they used to be in times of slow transportation and communication; they would form a vital part of the world at large, and would reach out to that world in a spirit of broader cooperation, learned on the field of actual, personal experience at home. For world brotherhood can hardly be developed except through this doorway of direct experience in brotherhood on a small scale first. It can hardly even be understood without at least a few small, model examples.

An Ideal Tested and Proved

Harmony and loving cooperation on a community-wide basis are not idle dreams. At Ananda Cooperative Village we have found that inner peace acts like lubricating oil on the machinery of human relations. Rarely are there any arguments among our members. Brotherhood here is a living reality, one which readily expands itself into a sense of kinship with all life. But basic to our success is the fact that our structure only *permits* individual unfoldment; it does not presume to ordain it.

If Yogananda's vision of the future is true, and in time many such intentional communities are founded around the world, governments will more easily tend to fit Thoreau's famous dictum, "That government is best which governs least."* For many of the regulatory functions of government will have been assumed by a harmonious and cooperative populace.

---

* *Civil Disobedience*

Chapter 12

WHEN WILL TRIALS COME?

To some extent they have come already. For several years the storm clouds have been gathering: even now, the first raindrops are falling.

Economically, we are caught in an inflationary rapids. In 1929, at the start of the great depression, there were eight paper dollars in circulation for every real, gold dollar in the United States Treasury. That proportion was already twice the limit originally set by law. By 1966 the ratio was thirteen paper dollars to every real dollar; by 1968, twenty-three to one; by 1971, twenty-five to one. And in the two years since then the inflationary spiral has been climbing faster than ever. The national debt at this time exceeds the sum of indebtedness of all other countries in the world. Interest alone on the U.S. national debt costs taxpayers more than $45,000 a minute—over eighteen billion dollars a year. And the figure keeps rising. Economically speaking, we are like a person running downhill faster and faster, in ever-greater danger that his legs will suddenly fail to keep up with him. Many

prominent economists and critics of our present
economy believe that America is tottering on the
brink of a massive depression, far worse than the one
of the thirties. Such men include Dr. Franz Pick,
the world's best-known authority on currencies and
gold; Harry Shulz, noted economic commentator;
Kevin P Phillips; William Partridge; Representa-
tive Wright Patman, chairman of the Banking and
Currency Committee of the U.S. Congress; Harry
Browne, top investment counselor and author of
How You Can Profit from the Coming Devaluation;
Robert L. Preston, author of *How to Prepare for the
Coming Crash*; and Don W. Mason, author of *In-
trinsic Values of Gold Coins*.

Other authorities have been predicting a world-wide
depression—not surprisingly, since most national
economies are tied closely together nowadays, and
since most also rely heavily on the supposed strength
of the U.S. dollar. The Mitsubishi Bank, one of
the leading banks of Japan, claims the possibility
of a worldwide depression within the next year or
two (from summer, 1973). The French economist
Jacques Rueff predicts a catastrophic world depression within a few years. And according to the popular Harry Shulz financial newsletter, Swiss banks this

summer (1973) began quietly removing from America gold holdings they'd been storing over there. (One wonders if perhaps a few people over there have decided things don't look too good over here.)

Rumors of Wars

On the international scene, too, the news is hardly cheery these days. The best one can say is that it isn't uniformly bleak. As war fades, or at least assumes less international importance, in Southeast Asia, tensions mount dangerously between Israel and the Arab countries, between Russia and China. Deep emotional commitments on the one hand to the Israeli cause, and a worldwide need for Arab oil on the other, make any conflict between Jews and Arabs a matter for global concern. Actual warfare between the two might easily embroil the major powers.

And China is said to be arming frantically to protect itself against an anticipated attack by Russia. Nor are these fears groundless. Russia has become all too conscious of the threat to her from China, with that younger communism nation rapidly developing nuclear power. Political thinkers in other countries have pointed out that it is to Russia's purely pragmatic advantage to demolish her enemy while the Chinese are still relatively weak. A national philosophy of atheism, moreover, would doubtless minimize any horror the Russian chiefs might feel at causing the deaths of a few million, or even a few hundred million, people.

Increasing Shortages

Shortages of oil and other fossil fuels, of food, of paper, of a growing list of other necessities—plastics, honey, cement, clothing materials (cotton, wool, leather, synthetic fibers), paints, antifreeze, glass—suggest cogently that we are in a time of rapidly mounting crisis. Part of the problem is that, after devaluation, other countries are able to pay better prices for American materials and products than these goods command domestically. Part of the problem, again, is simply that human need, and sheer greed, are outstripping our production capacities. Partly, too, the problem is that shortages of raw materials (oil, copper, zinc, phosphates) create shortages of goods in dependent industries. And partly the problem is that the rising cost of everything has discouraged many companies from spending to improve their production methods (or even their products), while concentrating heavily on advertising to increase their sales. The result is a growing demand, and higher prices, for increasingly shoddy goods that are becoming in ever shorter supply.

Consider our heavy dependence on mid-East oil supplies. Without those supplies, at least for the next few years until other sources can be developed, America's economy would virtually grind to a halt. Even now the Arab states are wondering out loud why they should continue sending oil to us, considering the precarious position of the dollar. Saudi Arabia, our biggest supplier, needs little in the way of goods from us in return, but counts on building up huge reserves of wealth in paper dollars for its own future development. Suddenly the dollar is devalued, and Saudi Arabia has ten percent less dollar wealth than it thought it had. One or two more devaluations, and we may expect Saudi Arabia to say, "We can't continue to send you our precious oil for increasingly worthless paper promises."

Suddenly—A New "Energy Squeeze"

That last paragraph appeared in the first edition of this book, before the Arab invasion of Israeli-occupied territory, and before the Arab cut-back on oil shipments to "uncooperative" nations. We may be sure that a major incentive to the Arabs for cutting off all shipments of oil to this country has been the fact they are not particularly happy anyway at the prospect of receiving increasingly unstable dollars in exchange for their precious "black gold." While the dollar has already been twice devalued in the last two years, the value of oil is certain to increase as the years go by.

Already there is talk in the Arab countries of converting their dollar holdings to some other currency. Should that happen, the flood of dollars on the world market would almost certainly result in yet another dollar devaluation. Experts are saying that, with or without such a flood, we'll anyway be forced to devalue further—much further.[*] Foreign money markets, they point out, have been growing increasingly restive over their mounting supplies of billions of insubstantial dollars. Demands for devaluation can hardly fail to continue until a more realistic ratio of dollars to hard currency is established.

With or without the shutting off of oil shipments from the Middle East, we have a serious energy

---

[*] See Harry Browne's book, *How You Can Profit from the Coming Devaluation*, Avon Books (New York City, September, 1971).

shortage rapidly developing in this country. For an industrial nation like ours, energy is the very foundation of our prosperity. Without it we go back to the hand loom and the hoe. The basic reason, in fact, for America's phenomenal wealth may be explained quite simply: cheap energy.

How Will It Happen?

As energy becomes more difficult to obtain, inevitably people will do less driving. Airlines and other travel companies will be forced to cut back on their flights, and therefore to lay off workers. Vacation resorts will receive fewer tourists, and will be hard hit in consequence. Many hotels and restaurants, depending on America's mobility for their survival, will be forced to close. With people driving less, fewer cars will be bought. The result: cut-backs and lay-offs in the automobile industry.

The lay-offs I'm referring to will affect not hundreds merely, but many hundreds of thousands of workers. And even these will be only a beginning. America is a leisure- and luxury-oriented society. Countless nonessential businesses exist only to cater to our free time, and to our endless eagerness for luxuries. It stands to reason that when people lose their jobs, their first concern will be to keep eating. Swimming pool companies, sporting goods stores, firms that sell travel campers, restaurants, and—well, the list is endless—will lose customers. Unable, consequently, to pay their own bills, many of them too will fold, creating resultant hardships on companies that have been relying, in turn, on *their* trade. None of the hardships would be so great were it not for the fact that America is in debt up to its eyebrows.* The modern life-style demands a continuous flow of money. Without this flow—which depends on stable incomes—everything must crumble like a house of cards.

Relatively little shocks have often sent ripples throughout the economy. We may predict, then, that any *big* shock will send *waves*.

If the Government realizes the extent to which its interference in the past has caused our present economic straits, and if (uncharacteristically) it decides this time to leave ill enough alone, we may expect

---

* Huge as the national debt is (greater than the sum of indebtedness of all other countries in the world), private indebtedness in this country is an incredible *four* times as large.

the present energy shortage to result at least in a recession in the months to come, leading more or less quickly, by a sort of domino effect, to a depression.

But since the Government's policy has been increasingly to subsidize everything and everybody, and since by now most citizens have grown to expect to be lovingly taken care of by their Father which is in Washington—and of course also, since politicians like to do the popular thing: I think we may expect the Government to step in and say, "We'll guarantee the wages of every unfortunate worker who gets laid off because of shortages." To pay these wages, of course, the Government will have to print more money, based on the usual empty promises.

And thus, with increasing shortages on the one hand, and a growing supply of money on the other, might well begin the dangerous spiral of runaway inflation.

People imagine that Government intervention can keep them secure. They little realize what a tightrope we are already walking, or the extent to which Government intervention has already undermined their security. The sad fact is that no country whose economic history is known has ever escaped runaway inflation that thought to print money with too little hard currency backing it.

The energy crisis is serious enough to threaten all of the above dangers even without the shut-off of Arab oil. *With* this shut-off, the danger is of course increased considerably.

When?

When may we expect trials to come? Actually, we are in the midst of them already. Government subsidies may help to postpone actual disaster for some time, but not without an ultimate price. For the longer it is postponed, the worse it must eventually be.

When a tree is rotten, it is difficult to know just when, or in what direction, it will fall. What I have outlined above is one scenario—an increasingly likely one. But the point to emphasize is the condition of the tree itself. The weaker its condition, the less external pressure will be required to topple it.

And, clearly, its condition is worse now—worse than ever before.

The Danger of Chaos

Should there be a crash in the stock market, or such a wave of inflation that prices must be changed daily to keep abreast of it,* the resulting confusion might well end in chaos.

I refer to chaos as a distinct possibility because even now, when people are still relatively prosperous, there is a growing violence in the air. In 1972, according to a Gallup Poll report published in January, 1973, one person in three living in big center-city areas was mugged, robbed, burgled, or had his property vandalized. In the suburbs during the same period, one person in five was so victimized. These dismal statistics don't imply that 1972 stood in any particularly shocking contrast to other recent years. It merely formed part of a curve that in recent decades has been sweeping more sharply upward every year. Crime in America today and in the world at large, has become a raging epidemic.

Worst of all, there is a sort of moral decay gnawing at the hearts of men, a rot of which crime, greed (the root cause of depressions), and international violence are but symptoms. Everywhere nowadays

* This sort of thing, as I mentioned earlier, has happened before.

one hears the doctrine: Life is meaningless; right and wrong are only terms of convenience; virtue is the disguise we ask others to wear, to prevent their selfish, animal interests from obstructing our own selfish, animal interests.

What will happen if our present, relative prosperity suddenly vanishes? Considering the prevalence now of crime, violence, and growing loss of moral direction, one wonders if large numbers of people won't completely lose their bearings during a time of financial disaster, when food becomes scarce, money loses its value, and jobs are impossible to come by. It is easy to imagine marauding gangs terrorizing the populace to get for themselves what they can.

There are too many imponderables to be able to predict with certainty when depression, or world war, or other calamities will strike in full force. But it seems evident to me that the above signs, coupled with the warnings of Paramhansa Yogananda, suggest imminent danger. As I write these lines (November 30, 1973) the banks, for the second time this autumn, are pushing the prime lending rate up towards 10%—a danger signal in the economy if ever there was one. The

Arabs and Israelis are talking of renewing their war. The energy crisis grows more serious every day. And the President's credibility has dropped to new lows, raising seriously the question of his administration's ability to cope with our mounting crises. Certainly, the time for preventive action is *now*. It is wiser to be prepared too soon than too late. And the danger signals are up and flashing already.

Chapter 13

HOW TO PREPARE

Greed is the root cause of all depressions. Indeed, folk wisdom enlarges on this concept, telling us that the love of money is the root of all evil.

And the wisdom of great seers in every culture gives us the logical corollary to that thought. Desirelessness, they say, is the root of all true happiness.

An ascetic in India was once upbraided by his well-to-do father for doing nothing to increase the family fortune.

"But I'm rich!" the son countered, joyously. "I have a home, a bed and bedding, a warm coat, protection when it rains, a good seat to sit upon, a table to eat at."

"That's little enough, I must say," grumbled the father. "But I'm told you live out of doors on a hillside. How is it that no one has seen all those possessions of yours?"

"Oh, but they have," replied the son, taking a large, thick piece of cloth from around his shoulders.

"Here is my shelter, my overcoat, my bed and bedding, my table, my seat for meditation. Why should I want more, when one piece of cloth suits all my physical needs to perfection?"

Obviously, for most people the alternative to the threat of financial ruin would not be to go out and live under a tree. But extreme examples at least help to illustrate which side of the golden mean is more golden. For while everyone praises moderation, some people, in the name of moderation, keep only one yacht, two cars, and three servants. But is it not better to be moderate in simplicity than to settle for being only moderately avaricious?

All a man really needs, materially speaking, is food, clothing, and shelter. The comforts he adds to these basics form part of what we are pleased to call "civilization." But civilization becomes a mockery when all one's energy is devoted to the acquisition of mere things, while heart, mind, and soul starve for their own natural nourishment. For love and wisdom, too, are basic human needs. Without them, our vaunted civilization is little more than a shiny, neat prison with automatic, self-locking doors.

"Americans," I've quoted Paramhansa Yogananda as saying, "were growing so rich they forgot God. But now God is performing an operation." If we are to survive the trials ahead, we must first develop a more sensitive appreciation for what it really means to be civilized: not to possess things, merely, but to expand our awareness and understanding. Material sophistication should be a stepping stone, not a widening abyss, to mental and spiritual development.

To prepare wisely for the times ahead, we should learn to be satisfied with less, and seek our strength more in ourselves and in God.

Don't equate civilization with cars and airplanes, but with wisdom. When you are secure in the fortress of your own soul, Yogananda said, you will be able to "stand unshaken amidst the crash of breaking worlds."

Right, appropriate action without understanding is like choosing the lucky number in a game of roulette. One never knows when his choice will be the right one. Therefore Yogananda stressed the importance of seeking understanding first.

Subordinate to that emphasis, however, he also recommended a few steps which, if kept in their proper proportion, might prove vitally helpful on an outwardly practical level. I'll list here those of his recommendations that I know, and throw in a couple of my own (numbers 4 and 8) for good measure.

1. Stocks

Don't depend on stocks for your security. The Master said, "There will be great fluctuations in the stock market, and then a depression the like of which you have never seen." If you have enough money in reserve to let your stocks ride through hard times, he suggested you invest only in blue chips, and avoid speculation.

Some people invest in stocks as a hedge against inflation. In fact stocks do tend to rise with the inflationary wave. If, however, the wave swells too fast, the value of stocks falls behind. And of course, once inflation collapses into a depression, the bottom falls out of the stock market, as out of just about everything else.

In the meantime the little investor, especially, will suffer all the anguish of the gambler desperately chancing everything on a few throws of the dice. Is it worth it? I think it wiser to withdraw from the market now. Better, as I said, too early than too late.

2. Savings Accounts

Keeping your money in savings may be just as unwise. In normal times both stocks and savings may be fine, but these are not normal times. Indeed, they've been abnormal for decades, but now at last the abnormalities, like a latent disease, are beginning to surface.

Even though savings accounts in this country are insured up to $20,000, the Federal Deposit Insurance Corporation has only $4 billion to cover a total of $313 billion in savings. Worse still, as Harry Browne points out in his book, *How You Can Profit from the Coming Devaluation*, "Virtually all of the insurance fund is used to finance the government's bonds. Only $6 million is kept in cash."* If a handful of small banks fail, newspapers around the country will print the reassuring news:

* Op. cit., p. 57.

All depositors were promptly paid by the Government. And depositors everywhere will breathe sighs of pure satisfaction, knowing that, with their federally insured savings, they've put their money (to quote a recent ad) "in exactly the right place."

But what if more banks and savings companies should fail? Enough of them certainly did during the last depression. There simply isn't enough insurance money set aside to cover such a disaster. The whole purpose of the Federal Deposit Insurance Corporation is to give people enough confidence in the system not to rush to withdraw their savings in a mass panic. Fair enough—perhaps. At least it props a chair, if somewhat precariously, against *one* of the doors to disaster. But what if there arise other reasons than sheer panic for a mass withdrawal of savings? Suppose inflation got so out of hand that people decided they'd better spend their money on something solid while they still could. Or suppose vast numbers lost their jobs, or depression tightened the flow of money: In either case, people's savings would be needed to pay their debts and meet their expenses. Panics result from loss of confidence. But loss of confidence isn't always the result of mere rumor.

The reason banks close when too many people close their accounts is that standard banking practice sanctions the issuance of several times more money receipts than the actual money they keep on hand. And modern banks, like everyone else, have vastly over-extended themselves.

Eventually, of course, the Government would pay off those insured deposits in banks that had failed. How? Quite simply, by printing vast quantities of paper dollars. But by that time you and millions of others would be wondering what to do with all that paper—use it to start a fire, when you can't afford to buy firewood?

Here then is a point to ponder: The present rate of savings withdrawals is unusually high, and appears to be going higher.

3. Checking Accounts

If the banks should close in large numbers as they did during the last depression, your checking account might be no safer than it would be in the hands of a robber.

I suggest you keep only as much money in your

checking account at the bank as you think you'll
need to meet your running expenses.

4. Solid Assets

You may want to investigate the possibilities of investing some of your money in solid assets. Americans *are* allowed to own gold in certain forms, and
there are no restrictions on owning silver. Books are
available on this subject: I recommend you buy and
study one or two of them carefully before investing.

Solid assets will help you particularly if inflation
gets out of hand. For as paper money loses its
buying power, your solid assets will gain power.
That is why, during the inflation that devastated
Germany in the Twenties, people invested wildly in
anything solid they could get: toasters, furniture,
books—anything, in the hope of having at least
something left to bargain with.

But I'm not suggesting investments as a means of
preserving your present life-style. Still less am I suggesting them as a way of riding a financial debacle
to new wealth. My true interest is to direct you towards what my guru said was the actual, though

subtle, purpose of the trials ahead: the discovery of a new, simpler, and more spiritual way of life. Therefore I want to stress above all, as he did, the following alternative:

5. Land

Again and again in public lectures Paramhansa Yogananda urged people to invest in real property. He wasn't proposing land as a money-making investment, but as a place to live on. Of course, he particularly stressed its value during a depression, but he hoped also that people would discover new norms in living close to nature, no longer dependent on the artificialities of our age, with its air conditioners, TV dinners, plastic proliferation, and endless stretches of freeways.

"Grow your own food," he urged people, "build your homes with your own hands, learn to live simply, and spend more time out of doors, renewing your contact with nature and with God."

So interested was he in every aspect of this new-age naturalism that he even detailed such simple, practical measures as constructing buildings out of materials that wouldn't require repainting every few years.

To him, going back to the land didn't mean rejecting modern civilization, but only correcting certain imbalances in modern progress: a tendency to mistake material ease for peace of mind, opulence for success, and confusion for happiness. But he approved of the modern inventive spirit. Often, in fact, he delighted in it, and actually came up with a number of inventive ideas of his own. Though spiritual, he was also completely practical, and held that these two principles should be combined in a higher, truer kind of practicality, a "balanced material and spiritual efficiency." To him, then, going back to the land meant making sensible use also of labor-saving machinery, and of modern, technical know-how. The essential provision was that the end be simplification, not further material involvement and dependency.

"It is quite all right to own possessions," he told people. "Just don't allow yourself to become possessed by your possessions."

He saw living close to nature as a step further along the pathway to true civilization, and not as a sort of

Rousseauesque neo-primitivism, where the mere fact of living among the trees would automatically transform world-weary sophisticates into "noble savages."

6. Cooperative Communities

If your are like most people, you might find it difficult to fend for yourself in the country. You may not know a joist from a stud, nor even a radish from a turnip. To build your own home might result in your spending the rainy seasons swimming from kitchen to living room, and from bedroom to bathroom, as though determined to outdo Rousseau's noble savage himself—going back, nostalgically, to a still more basic age and the unencumbered simplicity known by our aquatic ancestors.

To grow your own food, too, might prove a disagreeable alternative to simply gathering your weeds from a nearby city lot.

Therefore Yogananda suggested you join hands with a few friends and form a spiritual cooperative, buying enough land in the country to meet your group needs. You will find greater security in such unity than you would living alone. And each of you will go to the country equipped with certain skills, or with a chance to specialize in developing one set of skills while other members concentrate on developing others. In community, too, you will probably find greater stimulus for self-development than you would living alone.

For a practical guidebook to cooperative spiritual living, I humbly suggest my own book, *Cooperative Communities—How to Start Them, and Why.*

7. Act Now

As soon as you find it feasible, leave the city and move onto your own (or your community's) land. Learn, as I said, to live simply, to work with your hands, and to harmonize yourself with the rhythms of nature.

Especially if a depression comes, and even more especially if it comes suddenly, the cities may not be safe places to live in. Robbery, vandalism, and violence of all kinds are prevalent even today. Safety, certainly, is an added attraction to living together with others, as well as to living in the country.

But here, too, the main thing is to begin now to attune yourself to the spirit of the new age we are living in, and not to wait until forced to do so by dire necessity. The spirit of this age does not actually *demand* a return to the country. As Yogananda pointed out, if everyone were to move to the country, cities would only have to be built there to accommodate them. What the new spirit demands, rather, is a more simple, less cluttered and artificial way of life *wherever one lives*, a life based on human and spiritual rather than on material and institutional values. Voluntary cooperation, rather than selfish competition, will become more and more the accepted spirit in the decades to come.

Until a new principle is understood, however, and mentally digested, it is often necessary to apply it in its most obvious and easily understood form. Simple, spiritual living and voluntary cooperation are theoretically quite as possible in the cities as they are in the country. It is one's old mental associations with different patterns of living that make a new lifestyle, to practical purposes, so difficult to achieve.

Not only for one's own clarity of purpose, then, but also to set a clearer example to others, the development of the ideals I've outlined above would have the strongest impact if most such experiments were conducted in the simplicity of nature. And of course there remains, for city dwellers, as I have said, the special threat to their safety during chaotic times.

If, however, for any reason it is simply not feasible for you to leave your life in the city, then try at least to form a spiritual cooperative with friends of like mind where you live now. They will help you to achieve the inner balance you seek. And they will also provide you, and you them, with a measure of safety and security in time of need.

8. Stockpile Foods

Stockpile those foods which will keep for a long time: grains, powdered milk, alfalfa seeds, honey or sugar, soybeans. I never actually heard my guru make this suggestion, but it seems eminently practical in the light of what he did say. Study what the Mormons have done; they are specialists in this field.

The purpose in stockpiling basic foods is to lay in a supply during times of relative plenty, rather than wait until they become generally scarce and costly. To buy now would place less of a strain on available supplies later, when the pinch became widely felt. To gather and hoard supplies, however, during times of scarcity would in the long run be self-defeating. Rather, your stockpile of basic foods ought to be used then, for the care of others. For even considered selfishly, it is to everyone's advantage in times of trial to work cooperatively for the general welfare. It is indeed the insufficiency of this spirit in the first place that has brought us to our present economic predicament.

9. Already-Established Communities

During the pioneering stage of any movement the difficulties are always greater than later on, when experience has been gained, and when a certain measure of stability has been achieved. Cooperative communities are prophesied as an important social pattern for the future. At present, however, the pattern is so new that many groups, attempting sincerely to embrace it, have failed. Unfortunately for them, their utter inexperience coincides with those most crucial years in any undertaking—the first five.

Realizing from hard experience how difficult it can be for a new community to make it through the crucial first years, we at Ananda Cooperative Village hope to share what we've learned with others. To that end we have begun planning to found an Institute of Cooperative Spiritual Living, where people can come not only for study, but for active participation in community programs. Though at present this institute is still in the planning stage, everything else at Ananda has developed so quickly that the present plans, too, may well become a reality by the time our friends have adjusted themselves to considering it actually a part of our long-range goals.

But if the idea of starting a community yourself frightens you, and if you cannot envision anyone else in your present circle of friends starting one, why not consider joining some already-established and thriving community?

Here at Ananda we are working hard to prepare ourselves to receive new members in larger numbers during the critical times ahead, as well as perhaps to guide others in founding their own communities. The membership requirements at Ananda are fairly

strict, and will not suit everyone. Should they suit
you, perhaps this is where you'd like to come. If
not, why not look into one or more of the several
other communities that have been started success-
fully in recent years in America? There may even be
one near you.

10. Learn How to Meditate

Above all, whatever your religious beliefs, I would
urge you to learn the art of meditation. Attend
meetings at one of those churches which teach this
art, such as those of Self-Realization Fellowship. Or
come up to our Ananda Meditation Retreat.* You
will always be welcome here.

Study the Self-Realization Fellowship lessons on the
art of meditation, or my "Fourteen Lessons in Yoga,"†

---

* Instruction in meditation is now also available in person at any
of the Ananda communities Swami Kriyananda later founded in
the United States and Italy, at Ananda's many meditation groups
and teaching centers throughout the world, and through online
classes as well. —Publishers' note

† Swami Kriyananda subsequently retitled this book *The Art and
Science of Raja Yoga: Fourteen Steps to Higher Awareness.* Since 1974
he authored two other books on meditation specifically—*Meditation
for Starters* and the more comprehensive *Awaken to Superconscious-
ness*—and encouraged Ananda's presentation of meditation instruc-
tional materials online as well, at www.ananda.org. —Publishers' note

which are sent out by Ananda Cooperative Village.

Remember Paramhansa Yogananda's words: Those who follow this teaching (of inner, Self-realization) will be protected during the difficult times to come."

"A New World"

In all your preparations, don't lose sight of the long view. Live not in fear, but in hope, and in the security of God's love.

And above all, don't make the mistake of expecting this world ever to give you everything you want. It is that initial false hope that has led to widespread greed, from which have followed all the sufferings the human race has ever been heir to. As Paramhansa Yogananda said, "Do not seek perfection in this world. Seek it only in God." Human life is but a stepping stone to divine perfection.

The Master was once told by God in a vision: "I am your stocks and bonds. Dance of life and dance of death: Know that these come from Me, and as such, rejoice!" The final lesson of the trials on the Road Ahead will be man's need for the wealth of inner, spiritual awareness.

But Yogananda foresaw that humanity as a whole would approach this truth more nearly in the years to come than it has in countless centuries. Alas, that the approach must be through suffering! Indeed it needn't be, if men would only learn *now* to love one another. But however great the darkness in the tunnel we are so quickly approaching, we may take great comfort from the knowledge that at least the darkness will be temporary.

As the great Master Paramhansa Yogananda once said, of the light in the centuries beyond:

"*I prophesy:* You will see a new world!"

Appendix

QUESTIONS AND ANSWERS

Q. *Doesn't America's prosperity depend on people's faith in the economy? And isn't it only increasing the danger of a crash to predict one?*

A. According to modern economic theory—based as it is, not on gold, but on the nation's productivity—it doesn't matter what is used for money so long as people agree to accept it. If a government stipulates that paper bills are legal tender, and if people are willing to accept it as such, the economy should (we are told) float smoothly even with no gold backing it. The government need only balance the flow of paper money against the nation's productivity in such a way that there is neither a surfeit of currency (which would lower its value) nor an insufficiency of it (which would lower productivity) for there to be perpetual prosperity.

But in fact faith only sets the stage initially. It is people's faith in the currency that permits them to accept it. Whatever happens *after* they accept it has nothing to do with their faith. If too many paper dollars are floating around in ratio to the things they can buy, no amount of faith in those dollars will make them as valuable as they would be if they were scarce. Never was faith in the American economy stronger than in 1929, just before the crash.

No doubt paper can serve as money quite as well as gold, so long as everybody accepts it. Gold too, after all, has value only to the extent that people give it value. But the disadvantage of paper currency is that governments can print it so easily. No scouring the earth for scarce gold deposits; no laborious and costly mining: A few quick turns of the press, and billions of crisp, fresh paper bills can be created. The temptation is too great for most politicians to resist. By mere fiat they can create all the money, or simpler yet, promises of money, they need to finance huge, popular projects that will win them precious electoral votes.

The other side of this equation is the nation's productivity. Governments are strongly tempted also to tamper with productivity, to keep it in balance with the tampering they have already done with the money supply. Thus it is that a free economy gives a way gradually to a controlled one. The controls, moreover, are all on the people; there are fewer than ever on the leaders responsible for the trouble in the first place.

Q. *But isn't faith also important with respect to demand? As long as there is sufficient demand for things in relation to supply, can't the ratio of paper money to this supply be balanced out in the long run?*

A. This is indeed the hope of modern economic theorists: that people will want more and more, and that consequently more and more will be produced—enough, eventually, to offset the presently inflated dollar. Unfortunately, the banks' willingness to lend money they don't actually own—themselves borrowing, in effect, on the nation's future productivity—constitutes inflation too. Most of our paper money in fact consists not of actual, printed dollars, but of paper promises in the form of various kinds of debts. And private debts in America are four times as large as the national debt.

Surely, if one could be talked into wanting, and expecting eventually, an infinite number of goods, one might *hope* that the printing of paper money would stop somewhere short of infinity, leaving money still in short enough supply to be worth something as a means of exchange. But the presently increasing number of shortages belies this expectation. The problem with human desires is that they can be created even more easily than paper money. A nation's productivity is the only ponderous factor in this equation. All the forces in modern economics, therefore, operate on the side of inflation. The plain fact is, the longer the crash is delayed, the worse it will be.

Man was not meant to live more and more intensely for mere things. Nor is true civilization to be equated with the number of such things he can produce. To live simply, like the holy men of India, with no wants beyond the sheer basics—food, clothing, shelter—might indeed be the highest wisdom, for it would leave one time for more meaningful pursuits. If one starves oneself completely of the higher, spiritual demands of his nature, he gradually enters a state of such manic imbalance that eventual collapse is inevitable.

Q. *(January, 1974) The oil crisis presently is strengthening the dollar abroad. Does this fact alter your thinking on the future of the dollar in relation to other currencies?*

A. What we have here is, from all indications, a temporary situation. The dollar's present strength on the world market is due not to any intrinsic merit of its own, but merely to the fact that other countries are more dependent on Arab oil than we are. The relative strength of our position is like the bright prospects a fighter might face if his opponent suddenly caught pneumonia. The healthy fighter would not have grown any stronger. There might even, in the over-all situation, have been an actual loss, since the healthy one would probably find he had to expend less energy now to win.

In the international currency situation there has been no over-all gain as a result of the oil embargo. Indeed, far from really benefiting us, the embargo poses a serious threat to our own economy as well.

Q. *Did Paramhansa Yogananda say anything about the role of women in the times ahead?*

A. I myself never heard him say anything directly on this subject. A sister disciple, however, once reported to me certain things he had told her. I'm unable to quote her verbatim. Yet I submit with some confidence what I remember of her words, for they seem to me (judging from some of his remarks on related matters) the very sort of thing I think he *would* have said.

What he is reported to have said is that women will hold a much more important position in society in future than they have held heretofore; and that women will lead the way in bringing about a necessary balance in human affairs between reason and feeling, between wisdom and love.

Adding a personal interpretation of my own to his words, I believe he must have felt it would be due largely to the influence of women that humanity would come to embrace voluntary, as opposed to merely legislated, cooperation as one of the basic ideals in the new age.

A male-dominated society has always tended to over-emphasize the mere legalities of reform. Feeling is needed for reason's endless deliberations to be translated into dynamic action. In men, the Master often pointed out, reason is uppermost, and feeling hidden. In women, he said, feeling is uppermost, and reason hidden. Human nature starves for proper balance when either of these aspects is developed at the expense of the other. The deepest attraction between the sexes is not physical, but the instinctive longing in all mankind to bring reason and feeling, wisdom and love, into a state of natural balance and harmony.

Q. *Did Yogananda ever speak of the Second Coming of Christ?*

A. Yes. Often, in fact. But he reminded his listeners of the words Christ himself spoke: "Verily I say unto you, There be some standing here, which shall not taste of death, till they see the Son of man coming in his kingdom" (Matt. 16:28). And again he referred us to Jesus' words: "Verily I say unto you, *this generation shall not pass* till all these things (regarding the Second Coming) shall be fulfilled" (Matt. 24:34). In other words, as Yogananda saw it, the Second Coming was not prophesied as an objective, global event, but as an inner awakening in the souls of true, receptive disciples. This Second Coming has occurred, the Master said, in every century, in devotees who have responded to the eternal promise of Jesus: "Behold, I stand at the door, and knock: if any man hear my voice, and open the door, I will come in to him, and will sup with him, and he with me" (Rev. 3:20).

Jesus often rebuked his disciples for placing materialistic interpretations on his words. "My kingdom," he explained, "is not of this world" (John 18:36). The fulfillment he offered us was not an eternity imprisoned in a physical body—so inconvenient, if not suffocating, to the soul—but divine freedom in some more heavenly realm.

Paramhansa Yogananda also spoke of his own mission as being, in an outward sense, Christ's Second Coming. For it was, he told us, Jesus himself who had sent him to the West to remind people of the deeper, truer aspects of the New Testament teachings.*

Q. *Would you please give more details of Ananda Co-operative Village, mentioned in these pages?*

A. Ananda was founded in 1968, in the beautiful foothills of the Sierra Nevada in northern California. Until recently, it had about 330 acres of forest and farm land. In January, 1974, it acquired another 326 acres. The present number of full-time residents stands at about 115 persons, ranging in age from newly born to seventy years, the majority of adults being in their late twenties and early thirties.

Ananda grows an increasing proportion of its own food. It also supports itself by a variety of enterprises: records and publications (including the

---

* Kriyananda later wrote the book *Revelations of Christ*, in which he presented the teachings of Jesus Christ as proclaimed by Paramhansa Yogananda. —Publishers' note publication of this book), printing (for others as well as for ourselves), greeting cards, paintings, incense, artistic wild-flower jewelry, abalone jewelry, body oils, natural foods, firewood, medical instruments, dressmaking, tape recordings, honey, tree planting, vegetables, and outside lectures, concerts, slide shows, and dramatic presentations. Most of the businesses are privately owned. Services within the community presently include a car repair shop, road grading, a small dairy farm, a fruit and vegetable market, busing service to nearby Nevada City, a saw mill, a laundromat, and ice cream stand, occasional movies, carpentry, and various teaching positions in our grade and high schools, which cater also to students from outside the community.

Finally, and most important for non-residents, Ananda offers a year-round meditation retreat, with classes, devotional services, and an opportunity for spiritual inspiration and rejuvenation. Many hundreds of people every year take advantage of these retreat facilities.

In the planning stages also are an inexpensive health clinic and sanatorium, open to the general public, and an Institute of Cooperative Spiritual

Living. The purpose of this institute will be particularly to help people who want to start their own communities.

Membership requirements, and further details of our community life, may be found in my book, *Cooperative Communities—How to Start Them, and Why*.[*]

Publishers' Appendix

ON THE DIFFICULTY OF TIMING IN PROPHECY

The following passage was written by Swami Kriyananda many years after he published The Road Ahead. Because it addresses, and in so fascinating a way, a question that this book inevitably raises, we've chosen to include it here.[†]

Crystal Clarity Publishers

Imagine the windless surface of a dead sphere in space. Let's call it a planet, for its surface is solid. But there is no sun for it to revolve around. There are no stars anywhere: nothing to which this solitary sphere might be related.

Since comparisons are impossible, one couldn't say that our sphere was large or small, or moving one way or another, or even moving at all. In the absence of other heavenly bodies, it would be impossible even to determine the existence of space.

---

† The beginning of Chapter 14, "The Law of Transcendence," from *Out of the Labyrinth*, by J. Donald Walters (Swami Kriyananda), Crystal Clarity Publishers, 1988.

Let us now conjure into existence one other heavenly body: a sun, stationary above the planet's surface. Both spheres are motionless.

In the complete absence of movement, obviously, there can be no passage of time.

Let us now introduce movement. Imagine the sun rising in the east, arching over the planet, and setting in the west. Time, with this movement, is introduced into the picture. So far, however, it would be impossible to say, in terms of our earth time, whether this planetary day had encompassed a second, a year, or a billion years. Time would exist, but it would as yet have no relative meaning.

Next, let us imagine this planet as our own earth, teeming with all the restless activity to which we people of earth are accustomed: the heaving tides, rolling surf, scudding clouds, lightning flashes, and driving rain; the bright flowers and humble grasses nodding in the wind; the buzzing insects; the brief, swift flight of sparrows, and the slow circling of hawks; the hubbub of human enterprise; the heartbeats and breathing of men and animals; the life and death cycles of all living creatures.

Time, now, would have taken on relativity and would be filled with rich meaning. A day would have become an identifiable time span, very different from a year, from a billion years, and from the fleeting minutes and seconds by which we delude ourselves into imagining that life is long.

Finally, into this kaleidoscope of chronological relativity let us introduce one more factor: thought. Thoughts, for us, have the power to slow time down or to speed it up. Relative to the vibrations of thought, a minute might seem like an hour, or a day be condensed into the brevity of a few minutes.

I remember one morning in college sitting down to write a play. So deep was my concentration that I had the impression only minutes had passed, when I found to my amazement that I had to turn on the light, as the sun was setting. Nine and a half hours had flown by! Such is thought's influence on time.

Travelers commonly experience time very differently from the family members and friends they leave at home. A voyage of one month may seem to them, according to their own time sense, to have taken months.

It is movement which produces time. It may even be that movement and time are synonymous. Is it then movement also which produces space? Space without movement is a meaningless concept, certainly. Movement, rather than static positions in space, is what creates the essence of reality as we know it.

Here, then, is an interesting philosophical conundrum: If a clock is stopped, does it tell the correct time twice a day? Or is it never correct? Philosophically speaking, since time is inextricable from movement, one would have to say that the stopped clock never tells the correct time.

It is consciousness which determines how quickly time passes, since only consciousness attaches values to anything. But it is also consciousness *in motion*—the movement of thoughts, in other words—which makes this value judgment, which gauges objective movement in relation to subjective movement.

Suppose, now, that we were fully conscious, but without thoughts. Would all other movement cease, for us, to exist? Perhaps we would observe movement not as something that occurs in space, but as something that had already occurred: a completed cycle.

The potential energy for the completion of a pendulum's swing exists already before the pendulum is set into motion. We've suggested already in Chapter 12 that for anything to have appeared in the long evolutionary climb, it must have existed from the very beginning *as a potential*. Perhaps the same thing is true of movement.

Again and again in the utterances of the truly wise—that is to say, the great men and women of spiritual vision—we encounter the statement that time and space are only mental concepts. One thinks here of the answer Jesus Christ gave to the Pharisees: "Before Abraham was, I *am*."

A mind that held not the flicker of a moving thought would, on beholding movement, be faced with three alternatives: either to move mentally with that motion, and thus cease remaining motionless; or—but not really conceivably—to see it as a sequence of motionless positions; or else, to see it as an entire cycle, a completion, in which no movement had actually taken place at all, since the cycle existed already in its entirety from the moment of its projection.

A comparison might be made here to a large painting, the whole of which exists already, and can be seen in its entirety from the detached perspective of distance, while anyone standing close to it must take it in a section at a time, as his gaze passes over it in a broad sweep.

Perhaps this is the explanation for the phenomenon of prophecy, which defies common sense and yet has been demonstrated again and again to exist. A commonly reported feature of prophecy is the fact that those with the gift for it often err in the matter of timing. Their error is understandable, if their vision springs from levels of consciousness where movement, as such, doesn't exist, because its cycle is already seen as a wholeness.

"As a bright light shining in the midst of darkness, so was Yogananda's presence in this world. Such a great soul comes on earth only rarely, when there is a real need among men."

— His Holiness the Shankaracharya of Kanchipuram

Born in 1893, Yogananda was the first yoga master of India to take up permanent residence in the West.

Yogananda arrived in America in 1920 and traveled throughout the country on what he called his "spiritual campaigns." Hundreds of thousands filled the largest halls in major cities to see the yoga master from India. Yogananda continued to lecture and write up to his passing in 1952.

Yogananda's initial impact on Western culture was truly impressive. His lasting spiritual legacy has been even greater. His *Autobiography of a Yogi*, first published in 1946, helped launch a spiritual revolution in the West. Translated into more than fifty languages, it remains a best-selling spiritual classic to this day.

Before embarking on his mission, Yogananda received this admonition from his teacher, Swami Sri Yukteswar: "The West is high in material attainments but lacking in spiritual understanding. It is God's will that you play a role in teaching mankind the value of balancing the material with an inner, spiritual life."

In addition to *Autobiography of a Yogi*, Yogananda's spiritual legacy includes music, poetry, and extensive commentaries on the Bhagavad Gita, the *Rubaiyat* of Omar Khayyam, and the Christian Bible, showing the principles of Self-realization as the unifying truth underlying all true religions. Through his teachings and his Kriya Yoga path millions of people around the world have found a new way to connect personally with God.

His mission, however, was far broader than all this. It was to help usher the whole world into Dwapara Yuga, the new Age of Energy in which we live. "Someday," Swami Kriyananda wrote, "I believe he will be seen as the *avatar* of Dwapara Yuga: the way shower for a new age."

ABOUT THE AUTHOR

"Swami Kriyananda is a man of wisdom and compassion in action, truly one of the leading lights in the spiritual world today."
—Lama Surya Das, Dzogchen Center, author of *Awakening the Buddha Within*

A prolific author, accomplished composer, playwright, and artist, and a world-renowned spiritual teacher, Swami Kriyananda (1926–2013) referred to himself simply as close disciple of the great God-realized master, Paramhansa Yogananda. He met his guru at the age of twenty-two, and served him during the last four years of the Master's life. He dedicated the rest of his life to sharing Yogananda's teachings throughout the world.

Kriyananda was born in Romania of American parents, and educated in Europe, England, and the United States. Philosophically and artistically inclined from youth, he soon came to question life's meaning and society's values. During a period of intense inward reflection, he discovered Yogananda's *Autobiography of a Yogi*, and immediately traveled three thousand miles from New York to California to meet the Master, who accepted him as a monastic disciple. Yogananda appointed him as the head of the monastery, authorized him to teach and give Kriya Initiation in his name, and entrusted him with the missions of writing, teaching, and creating what he called "world brotherhood colonies."

Kriyananda founded the first such community, Ananda Village, in the Sierra Nevada foothills of Northern California in 1968. Ananda is recognized as one of the most successful intentional communities in the world today. It has served as a model for other such communities that he founded subsequently in the United States, Europe, and India.

FURTHER EXPLORATIONS

CRYSTAL CLARITY PUBLISHERS

If you enjoyed this title, Crystal Clarity Publishers invites you to deepen your spiritual life through many additional resources based on the teachings of Paramhansa Yogananda. We offer books, e-books, audiobooks, yoga and meditation videos, and a wide variety of inspirational and relaxation music composed by Swami Kriyananda.

See a listing of books below, visit our secure website for a complete online catalog, or place an order for our products.

crystalclarity.com
800.424.1055 | clarity@crystalclarity.com
1123 Goodrich Blvd. | Commerce, CA 90022

ANANDA WORLDWIDE

Crystal Clarity Publishers is the publishing house of Ananda, a worldwide spiritual movement founded by Swami Kriyananda, a direct disciple of Paramhansa Yogananda. Ananda offers resources and support for your spiritual journey through meditation instruction, webinars, online virtual community, email, and chat.

Ananda has more than 150 centers and meditation groups in over 45 countries, offering group guided meditations, classes and teacher training in meditation and yoga, and many other resources.

In addition, Ananda has developed eight residential communities in the US, Europe, and India. Spiritual communities are places where people live together in a spirit of cooperation and friendship, dedicated to a common goal. Spirituality is practiced in all areas of daily life: at school, at work, or in the home. Many Ananda communities offer internships during which one can stay and experience spiritual community firsthand.

For more information about Ananda communities or meditation groups near you, please visit **Ananda.org** or call **530.478.7560**.

THE EXPANDING LIGHT RETREAT

The Expanding Light is the largest retreat center in the world to share exclusively the teachings of Paramhansa Yogananda. Situated in the Ananda Village community near Nevada City, California, the center offers the opportunity to experience spiritual life in a contemporary ashram setting. The varied, year-round schedule of classes and programs on yoga, meditation, and spiritual practice includes Karma Yoga, personal retreat, spiritual travel, and online learning. Large groups are welcome.

The Ananda School of Yoga & Meditation offers certified yoga, yoga therapist, spiritual counselor, and meditation teacher trainings.

The teaching staff has years of experience practicing Kriya Yoga meditation and all aspects of Paramhansa Yogananda's teachings. You may come for a relaxed personal renewal, participating in ongoing activities as much or as little as you wish. The serene mountain setting, supportive staff, and delicious vegetarian meals provide an ideal environment for a truly meaningful stay, be it a brief respite or an extended spiritual vacation.

For more information, please visit **Expandinglight.org** or call **800.346.5350**.

ANANDA MEDITATION RETREAT

Set amidst 72 acres of beautiful meditation gardens and wild forest in Northern California's Sierra foothills, the Ananda Meditation Retreat is an ideal setting for a rejuvenating, inner experience.

The Meditation Retreat has been a place of deep meditation and sincere devotion for over fifty years. Long before that, the Native American Maidu tribe held this to be sacred land. The beauty and presence of the Divine are tangibly felt by all who visit here.

Studies show that being in nature and using techniques such as forest bathing can significantly reduce stress and blood pressure while strengthening your immune system, concentration, and level of happiness. The Meditation Retreat is the perfect place for quiet immersion in nature.

Plan a personal retreat, enjoy one of the guided retreats, or choose from a variety of programs led by the caring and joyful staff.

For more information or to place your reservation, please visit **Meditationretreat.org**, email Meditationretreat@ananda.org, or call **530.478.7557**.

THE NEED FOR SPIRITUAL COMMU-
NITIES AND HOW TO START THEM
Swami Kriyananda

Swami Kriyananda's network of Ananda communities has been hailed as the most successful in the world. Whether you are interested in communities from a philosophical perspective or a practical one—and wish to form your own or join with others in doing so—this book will bring you hundreds of helpful insights into the process—starting a community, making it prosper even in difficult times, and seeing it continue into a bright future.

OUT OF THE LABYRINTH
For Those Who Want to Believe, But Can't
Swami Kriyananda

The last hundred years of scientific and philosophical thought have caused dramatic upheavals in how we view our universe, our spiritual beliefs, and ourselves. *Out of the Labyrinth* brings fresh insight and understanding to this difficult problem. The author lays out a new approach to spirituality that both solves the problem of meaninglessness and champions the possibility of human transcendence and divine truth.

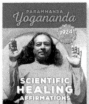

SCIENTIFIC HEALING AFFIRMATIONS
Paramhansa Yogananda

This reprint of the original 1924 classic by Paramhansa Yogananda is a pioneering work in the fields of self-healing and self-transformation. He explains that words are crystallized thoughts and have life-changing power when spoken with conviction, concentration, willpower, and feeling. Yogananda offers far more than mere suggestions for achieving positive attitudes. He shows how to impregnate words with spiritual force to shift habitual thought patterns of the mind and create a new personal reality.

Added to this text are over fifty of Yogananda's well-loved "Short Affirmations," taken from issues of *East-West* and *Inner Culture* magazines from 1932 to 1942. This little book will be a treasured companion on the road to realizing your highest, divine potential.

WHISPERS FROM ETERNITY
A Book of Answered Prayers
Paramhansa Yogananda
Edited by his disciple, Swami Kriyananda

Many poetic works can inspire, but few have the power to change lives. These poems and prayers have been "spiritualized" by Paramhansa Yogananda: Each has drawn a response from the Divine. Yogananda was not only a master poet, whose imagery here is as vivid and alive as when first published in 1949: He was a spiritual master, an avatar.

He encouraged his disciples to read from *Whispers from Eternity* every day, explaining that through these verses, he could guide them after his passing. But this book is not for his disciples alone. It is for spiritual aspirants of any tradition who wish to drink from this bountiful fountain of pure inspiration and wisdom.

THE WISDOM OF YOGANANDA
series

The Wisdom of Yogananda series features writings of Paramhansa Yogananda not available elsewhere. These books capture the Master's expansive and compassionate wisdom, his sense of fun, and his practical spiritual guidance. The books include writings from his earliest years in America, in an approachable, easy-to-read format. The words of the Master are presented with minimal editing, to capture the fresh and original voice of one of the most highly regarded spiritual teachers of the twentieth century.

MORE SELECTED OFFERINGS